Body of Evidence

Body of Evidence

poems

Kathleen Ellis

GRAYSON BOOKS
West Hartford, Connecticut
graysonbooks.com

Contents

Acknowledgments

Grateful acknowledgment is made to the editors of the following chapbooks and anthologies who first published versions of these poems:

Outer-Body Travel (Finishing Line Press, chapbook, 2017): "Holding the Breath," "Treading Water"

Rumors, Secrets, & Lies (Anhinga Press, anthology, 2022): "Early Warning Signal," "Shush, Don't Tell!," "Vitruvian Woman"

Vanishing Act (CC Marimbo Press, chapbook, 2007): "Ghost Child"

Wait: Poems from the Pandemic (Littoral Press, Portland, Maine, anthology, 2021): "How You Dressed for the Pandemic"

I am also grateful to poets Ellen Goldsmith and Claire Millikin for their close readings and comments on multiple drafts of many of these poems.

And a special thanks to RW Estela, who populates many of these poems, for his astute advice in the final stages of this book's completion.

Entering

The day before and a year after. To be born in the winter after Pearl Harbor is to be lost in the body of war. The month of Pleiades, visible from dusk to dawn. I place my body in the cluster of stars.

The world is hard to enter, harder to leave behind.

The Spanish Flu

My mother was born without a body. At least, that's what my grandmother said. I always wondered why my mother was born at home—was it the Spanish flu or that her mother was a Christian Scientist? Before she died in her eighties of septic shock, she went into a coma where there is no body, where nobody bleeds.

Before Hiroshima

During the Depression, my father is nineteen, his family on relief, when he spends two years constructing Camp Tule Lake before it becomes a relocation camp. George Takei is five when soldiers arrive at his L.A. home in 1942 and take him far away. Though not as far as the *Starship Enterprise* will. Takei's family is relocated to Arkansas, and then west to Tule Lake. I am fifteen when my family visits Tule Lake, its buildings still standing.

My father weeps as his fingers clutch the barbed-wire fence.

Body Parts I

I move at the speed my father swam from the Navy end of Alameda toward Treasure Island. Sailors are combing the beach, where my father teaches me how to breaststroke. When he was a boy, the bay was filled with sewage, and this was his stroke for dodging the undesirable. My father tells me to look at the city across the bay, look at the aircraft carriers heading into the post-War Pacific clean-up. *Do not look back.* I'm almost five and topless, and it is years before I will cover my chest.

For now, my father is teaching me the breaststroke, what to look out for.

False Alarm

We're eight and reading from *Science and Health* by Mary Baker Eddy in a circle at Sunday School, when a car backfires outside. The teacher thinks it's for real and makes us hide under our seats. She hushes us, but we can't resist the giggles. She's waiting for the all-clear that never comes.

Somebody raises a hand from under a seat and asks, "Did you think we were going to die?"

Ghost Child

When there was an earache
but no earache

(no, this never happened)

When there were measles
and whooping cough

and my palms were clasped
awkwardly together

and my mother was on the phone
with her mother, the practitioner,

I felt the shape of the Word
made stone inside my chest

And circling that terrible desire
to escape—I am not certain whether

inward or outward—
my mouth had opened wide

for the breath flying out of the body.

Early Warning Signal

It's summer on Alameda, and from the dankness of his garage, my next-door neighbor beckons me in to see the doll he's working on. Leon, the doll repairman, replacing body parts. First one leg, and then the other. He takes his hand and rubs it over the legs and into the narrow crevice of the body. Pops them back in, as if no one will ever know. *Shush, don't tell!*

Whose body? Whose legs?

After he's killed in a hit and run, a lion shadows my dreams.

Into Thin Air

I reach for the body and find it dispersed into thin air. The stars don't help. I know they are hiding something, the 10,000 things of the *Tao*. If I am not body, how can I speak or breathe? If I am not somebody, where do my feet go each morning? How do I know where I am without the compass of my brain?

Why does Emily say, "I am afraid to own a body...Profound— precarious property"?

You Are My Lucky Star

As we tap dance across the stage, a wave of nausea overwhelms me, but I do not fall. The dark audience is bodiless, only white and brown faces bobbing up and down with the music of the stars and our clumsy footwork. I look and look for a face I know, but I am nine, and the only face I recognize is the custodian's in the light of the exit door. On the way home, I ask my parents where they were sitting, and my father says they were late.

It is only then I take off my tiara of stars, ride all those miles home in silence.

Where No One Has Gone Before

Years before *Star Trek*, I clumsy together a Quaker Oats box pinhole planetarium. After I poke the pattern of stars into the disk of their constellation, I take the box and flashlight into the yard and lie in wait for the sky to darken. When I shine my light into the box, there is the cluster of Pleiades outlined against the sky.

In the night air, I am a starship hunting for my seven sisters.

3rd Grade, Encinal Avenue

Across the middle strip, my friend lives in the upstairs of a house. Each day we walk to school together. After school, we play two games of hopscotch, and then I cross the strip to my house. My friend is Black.

One night, sirens wake me to screams across the strip. Policemen carry a stretcher down the steps, as people gather, blaming the upstairs family for ruining the neighborhood. That's when I see my friend in tears. As her brother bleeds to death, we embrace until we are pulled apart.

The next week, they move away.

ABCs of Erasure

I am learning to vacate the body. The absence of body is a memory of body, a kind of lingering with the eraser dangling from one hand. I fear I've forgotten the body, left it behind somewhere. As a child, I stayed behind at the bayside watching the hermit crabs. To protect their exoskeletons, they trade in their tight-fitting shells for scavenged ones.

Or they risk being defenseless.

My Mother, Reading the Daily Lesson in Solitude

My mother has locked herself in her bedroom, and we've been ordered not to let a pin drop. Forty minutes later she emerges, silent but beatific. Still in her robe, she answers our questions with an eerie smile. She does not make us feel happy. She makes us afraid.

What is she not telling?

4th Grade, Duck & Cover

Every week we practice: Drop face down. Close eyes. Put your arms under the body and stay beneath your desk. Remain face down until the blast wave passes. Check for injury and prepare to resume living.

We hurry home as the siren blasts into the crosswalk where there are no guards, past the church with its doors wide open, and down the six long blocks of the neighborhood, wondering who or what is following.

6th Grade, Science Class

When the teacher assigns a project on human cells, he motions for me to leave the room. I head for the library to read about whales— their huge bodies, titanic heads, blowholes spouting breath into vapor. They can stay underwater for over an hour.

Instead of reading more, I draw a picture of a girl with a sharp-edged fluke, holding her breath for what seems like forever.

Holding the Breath

Sometimes I swim out to the farthest reaches.

I float with what I was
                and with the missing body
                                on the water of what I am.

And sometimes I swim beneath myself.
                Then I hold my breath
                                in the body of what I'm not.

But there's still another body
                in which I'll dive into the center
                                as if this were the only one there is.

Mammalia

I know a lot about the whales
    of the world
        as they were the only mammals

I was allowed to study as a child. The blues, humpbacks, fin whales,
    and lastly, the grays, those great long-distance migrators
        I cheered on from a cliffside at Mendocino.

But now, that slippery body on my chest needs to be released
    before it stifles my heart and lungs. For now, I've had enough
        of you and your bigger-than-thou attitude.

Not that I'd want you to fall back into the ocean and disappear.
    You are the only mammal I know by heart,
        your back-bending dives displaying your long,

white flippers, your blowhole bursting with air and water,
    water and air, those eerie songs you keen as you serenade
        each other on your way to the Baja lagoons.

What do you see in me? A woman who knows your body
    better than my own. Forbidden to turn the pages of *Gray's*
        Anatomy, I search your eyes for guidance.

At the aquarium, I wander to the ocean-view deck to watch you
    dive and breach, slapping your fins for the journey south,
        as I applaud the language we hold in common.

What do you see in us? Both vertebrates.
    Both of us holding our own in air and sea,
        back-boned, mammalian, warm-blooded

your body
closest to my own

Homo Ludens

All arms and legs, my swim coach teases me at thirteen. Neck of the
woods, arms of the law, over my dead body. I'm in over my head, but
I'm really just pulling your leg. As a rule of thumb, we *do* see eye to
eye. And now I'm ready to wash my hands of figures of speech, since
I'm always confusing them. But I am by nature a gaming animal,
Homo ludens, the body playing the mind, the mind playing the body.

All eyes, ears, nose, and throat.

Homo Faber

I'm fourteen and learning the names of the body parts in Spanish. What do you see through masculine eyes (*los ojos*)? What do you taste with a feminine mouth (*la boca*)? And what of the hand (*la mano*)? It's feminine, but its ending in *o* is not. The hands so uniquely human, unto themselves. Ambivalent, like libido, which is also feminine.

Homo faber: we make ourselves with our own two hands.

Treading Water

When I was a girl

I swam out of the body
whose image dives again and again

into the center
of the widest ocean.

I made myself weightless
on purpose for this entering into

blue the first color.
And darker still beneath my fins

my legs appearing and disappearing,
treading water.

Asana

As if it has something to defend, the body resumes its upright position.

You Are Not Who You Think You Are

According to a recent study, forty-three percent of our everyday actions are habitual. The beginning of you each day is already known by this body of you. Yet it is *not* you. More than half of you is still waiting to know what to accept, what to reject, how to act in this world.

More than half of you is becoming someone else.

Letter to My Body

I dream of you, body,

as if you are a friend

I have yet to meet.

I dream of you, body,

as if you are mine

in an alternate universe.

I dream of you, body,

as if you've always known

you're my one and only heartthrob.

In my dream, you turn

your back on me

and walk away.

When I wake beside you,

I do not blame you

for wanting to be free.

Condolences

All through childhood, my grandmother reminds me I have no body. No body to suffer, to ache, to know pain or death. When she dies in the 1960s, there is no body in her casket. At the service, the man with the kindly eyes rattles off all the good she's doing in her life in the present tense.

No one approaches the casket. Nobody checks to make sure.

Old Zen Buddhist Joke

Says the Master to his pupil: "Do you understand you don't really exist?"

Body Parts II

The body is a landscape bordered by the bay on one side and foothills on the other. When I watch the troopships duck under the bridge from Oakland on their way to Indochina, I think of you. You are not the boy who's going to have your head blown off in 'Nam. The boy named Larry (you have a name) who sat near me in orchestra. I on strings, you on drums.

I've mixed you up with someone who no longer exists.

What the Body Knows

My eyes know things my ears don't know.

My arms know things my legs don't know.

My mouth knows things my mind doesn't know.

What the body knows is the distance between us.

I know you by the stars in your throat

and the shoreline in your footsteps.

Lunula

Little moon. Crescent fingernail moon
in all its disguises.

When I learned the name for fingernail
in Spanish is *uña*,

I knew there's more to you than meets the eye.
Half-moon. Lunula. Original lullaby.

In all your disguises, you are always feminine,
always remaking yourself.

You are an *unguis*, a keratin structure
at the end of a digit.

Claw. Hoof. Talon.
Evolved from the nails of primates

and hooves of running mammals.
you are the rounded shadows,

and there is no one word
that does you justice.

You are closest to the skin,
the free edge of the body,

always rising, always halfway
in bright migration.

War on Polio

1954. And someone said. And someone asked. And someone wanted to know. And someone knew the only way to end this was by rolling up your sleeve. And the girl on the corner, and then the boy next door, and then we were surrounded by crippled legs and backs. And then my mother—which we didn't know until years later. And we kept on turning in our exemption cards.

1966. And twelve years later, I'm standing in the student plaza, where people are lined up for sugar cubes. My friend says we're next. And he asks, you *did* have the vaccine as a girl, didn't you? And someone holding a small cup offers. And I say *No.* And my friend shuns me for a week.

Interim

Once adrift,

apart from you,

I begin to claim this

body of blood, flesh, and

bones I have come to resemble.

Vitruvian Man, Squaring the Circle

You were a conundrum once,
an ███████ ancient problem Vitruvius posed
in the first century B.C., the one da Vinci
nearly solved centuries later.

You were the man of arms and toes
stretched ███ to the periphery of the circle,
or was it the edges of the square?

You were among the █████ models who posed
for Leonardo, ██████████████████████
███ standing naked hour after hour
in the dusty studio.

It was you who █████████████████ crept into the artist's hand,
curling your hand around his pen
and placing the fixed point of his compass

on your navel, the center of the universe.
And it was you who █████ peeked at the work in progress
during ███████ breaks, never knowing
the extent of Leonardo's erasures.

Vitruvian Woman

I'm lying on my back at the gynecologist's office, bare feet in the stirrups, legs clamped tight. *Open wide,* orders the surly man in the white jacket. As always, I resist. *Focus on something else,* he says in his doctor voice.

I think of Vitruvian Man stretched spread eagle, and I begin my silent rant about the perfect body, mirror of nature. I leave the gods out of it.

Think of it as a geometry problem, chimes in Vitruvius, *sotto voce.* It's all about proportion, squaring the circle, and returning to the umbilical.

The burly man's still trying to pull apart my legs. *Enough!* I rise from the table and take my body back.

The Dream of Edward Teller as a Grizzly Bear

When I was a newlywed, we moved to New Mexico where the land was forever. Those curious clouds that grew and grew and then abruptly disappeared. *There's nothing but horizon,* I said. *Nothing to fear,* you said. There were also mountains that captured the clouds each night and released them at dawn. Once, we drove into those mountains to see Oppie's lab at Los Alamos, and then took a side trip to Bandelier where the sheer cliffs housed human beings for over a thousand years.

That night I dreamed I was stalked by Edward Teller in a cloud chamber. He became my fears and the song of my thoughts like the soft padding of slippered feet. He became the absence inside me, a faint sensation, tiny claws beginning to sink into gut and groin. It's that feeling I came to define as being alive. I could see he was nearly blind and barely able to walk, and yet he could rise on his hind legs, roaring that insatiable roar in his guttural accent, clawing the air that rose and mushroomed out of sight.

Body Politic

We are laying our bodies down in public places,
learning to speak between the lines.

We are the news of the world in sound bites,
the falling man from the North Tower.

We are the woman who walks into a loaded rifle
of a boy soldier in 1980s Guatemala.

We are the colonized body, the exploited body,
the body ravaged with virus, the migrant body

escaping violence. We are the body of a country
waking every day with sorrow in the heart.

Chrysalis

A poem begins whether it wants to or not.

Just like a body begins without knowing where

it is headed. This is the edge I live on, the body

about to make its cameo appearance.

Where the Body Makes No Shadow

Solar Eclipse. Midday, I'm standing on a cobblestone street in Guanajuato, where the body casts no shadow. I feel naked, only halfway human as I turn around to find nobody else. Only a few stray dogs. Frightened women have fled indoors to escape the eclipse, which superstition says will cause their babies to be born with tails.

I am taking my chances with the world.

What Is Buried in the Backyard

Mexico. What is buried are bones, ashes, crucifixes scattered helter-skelter. My friend's an anthropologist, so she knows legit from illegit. I'm amazed she's allowed to dig up remains of tortured Judaizers, witches, and mulattos. What's left of them. When I leave her home, full of ceramic dogs exhumed from Colima gravesites, I pick up my pace. I'm walking uphill, past the stone fountain for the Virgin of Guadalupe. Soon I'm running along the cobbled street. The stones dig into my sandaled feet.

I fall and pick myself up, shaking off the dust of four centuries.

Alias Dictus

Alias, a.k.a. *Alias dictus*. A fictitious name assumed temporarily.

*

Anthropologists once thought some people were so "primitive" they didn't use names. Since they didn't know them well enough, they didn't know the taboo that names be kept secret from strangers.

*

In 1911, when Ishi, the last of his tribe, emerged from the forests of northern California, he refused to reveal his name. Alfred Kroeber named him Ishi, which means "man" in the Yana language. In Yahi culture, tradition demanded he not speak his name until introduced by another Yahi.

None had survived the genocide in the 19th century.

*

When I visit the *curandera* in the backstreets of San Miguel, she cannot pronounce my name, so she calls me Caterina. Her only language is Otomí, and her daughter interprets in Spanish what the *bruja* says. Stooped from a dowager's hump, she moves her hands around my body in places I feel pain. Her daughter prepares a bundle of dried herbs for me to mash and spread on where it hurts.

When she sees me staring at her mother's curved spine, she tells me she's cured thousands and carries their burdens on her back.

*

Alias (Latin). A term to indicate a person is known by more than one name.

*

Recipients of DACA must use the names on their birth registration documents. In Spanish-speaking countries, two last names appear on the documents. Even where the person only used one surname (usually the father's), they're forced to use both, creating a disparity in matters like credit ratings.

*

Freud says mispronunciation of your name amounts to a distortion of your identity. As a child, my teachers mispronounced my surname and classmates taunted with Clunk, Cough, Uncouth.

When did I take my grandmother's maiden name as my own?

*

After my mother's body died, I did not know how to mourn. How do you mourn someone who hasn't died? I have the card that pinpoints where her ashes were strewn into the bay, but no body to say she lived or died.

After my mother's body died, we grew closer and got along better.

Body of Evidence

The evidence begins to mount,
the sheer bulk of it.
I pile it up like unfinished
business, waiting
for the body of your body
to reappear.

In your closet
I find the stacks
and stacks of Bibles
and worn-out copies
of *Science & Health.*

The pages are dog-eared
where you touched them last.
I run my fingers over
your perfect signatures
on the title pages.
You, again and again
and again.

The Falling Man

We rush   to know you
name you
The urge is
to look away,
freeze-framing
your body
in mid-air
between the
towers
~~Stripped of~~
~~your name~~
~~but not your~~
~~number~~

Touch and Go

I touch everything that matters. Nouns, pronouns, body parts. When I climb to the top of Half Dome, the valley below is tempting. I want to lean over and touch the frigid water of the Merced River below. I want to smooth my hand along the face of El Capitan. I want to try a few touch-and-goes, swooping down, then landing and taking off again. That girl's bruise on her shin when she fell on the trail. That man's bicep bulging out of his t-shirt. This gnarled juniper clinging to life between the granite cracks. I want to touch them all.

I want to touch the world that has knocked me sensate.

Kiss and Tell

I don't remember

my first kiss.

To know human lips

are made for kissing

is to know more nerves

are involved than all

other body parts.

My lips open and close

forming an invitation

Come as you are

Come willingly

ready to release

your endorphins

meeting across

35,000 years

of being human.

Heart Condition

Knowing the cold, hard facts about glaciation doesn't mean we accept the wearing away of the coast we live on. I'm winding my way beside the Penobscot River, taking in the canopy of trees and parts per million of carbon in the air and the river rising and falling. When I reach the dam, the river plunges into its massive tremors.

There's a physical condition called broken-heart syndrome. It's caused by an emotional reaction to lost love, triggering a surge of hormones. One theory is if your heart's damaged, the repair of the injury requires stem cells. However, if the damage is stress-related, you can't repair your heart.

We prepare for the clamor of the melting ice sheet. We listen back into the Laurentide, its stressed arteries carrying the burden of loss, how this heart in which we live is the future of all its past.

Body Parts III

Mother tongue

Tip of the tongue

Skin of the teeth

Bundle of nerves

Head in the sand

Chip on the shoulder

Hairy eyeball

Hand over fist

Head over heels

Heart on your sleeve

Stiff upper lip

Rule of thumb

Sleight of hand

Scruff of your neck

Warts and all

Connecting in the Time of Pandemic

We haven't spoken in months, and now we're on the phone talking about time. The time we've lost, the time we can't keep track of, time as alternate reality. I tell you the Keck Observatory has discovered the most distant quasar known. The images show it 670 million years after the Big Bang, or more than thirteen-billion light years away. The photo of the two ecstatic astronomers bumping beer mugs makes them look like covert lovers. My thoughts stray far afield. Keck, my mother's maiden name. She has been dead since 2005, which seems like light-years.

Meanwhile, I want to keep you on the line, but we've lost our connection.

Love in the Time of COVID

For RW

After you visit your mother who has tested positive, I tiptoe around you as though you are contagious. I imagine you wrapped in a Hazmat suit making your way to the ward where your mother lies struggling for air. At first, she's confused about who you are. You are the body of her body, the one she has always loved.

Years ago, we met by chance in a rehearsal for *Ion*, translated by H.D. You played Hermes, wrapped in a plastic shower curtain toga. Hidden from the audience, I read H.D.'s notes from an upstairs platform. I/you. And now, we go to sleep in one body and wake up in another. Sight unseen.

How You Dressed for the Pandemic

In memory of L. C. (1846-1919)

Not everyone was thinking about how to dress
for the Spanish flu.

It didn't occur to you to choose between a gauze mask
or a veil of fine mesh and chiffon.

It wasn't the money. Myron, my great-grandfather,
Tax Collector of Alameda County,

would have bought you anything, Lizzy.

Outliving him, you survived the War at home,
wearing black for your own dead.

Now your choices were your own.

Did you poke holes in the mask to smoke?
There are no photos to prove otherwise.

Or were you a member of the Anti-Mask league,
or thinking of how to dress for the liberation?

And after you died in the third wave in 1919,
were your ashes strewn into the bay?

Or are they in a niche with a flowery scene
on a drawer at the Columbarium?

Here, stand in the light, so I can dress you.
Nothing to hide. Nothing to fear.

Come to claim what is ours—this mask I wear
that has no memories   but your absence.

Lines for the Pandemic

As if the distance measured in light-years
is the same distance our blood travels
through the universe of the body.

As if you and I are two lines in the same plane.
And if we intersect at more than one point,
we must be the same line.

As if honeybees have decided among themselves
to die younger and younger
at their own expense.

As if everything begins and ends as a simple dot
in space, all of us bee-lining
for the nearest exit.

As if these unending lines of cars
waiting for the drive-through testing
are witness to our enormous appetite.

When our bodies are full, we are amiable.
When they are not, we shrink into
total colony collapse.

Testing Positive

The job of a person is to stay alive.
Aristotle said it best: the job
of anything is to flourish.

Acorn: Oak tree
Cygnet: Swan
Calf: Whale
Human: Being

How our bones and limbs
outlast us.

And how I miss the avocado seeds
I nurtured as a girl, each of us
branching out.

Life is growing,
and not-so-life forms
are replicating in the back
of my throat and lungs,

this virus hiding out,
as if it were safe
to grow and flourish.

Shush, Don't Tell!

Back then, I didn't think it was fine—
but I knew there was
no other choice.

Back then, in the mid-sixties,
what crossed my mind
was I was unable,

when my own life was coming
into its own, a real job
in the city

and crossing any distance
between then and now
is admitting

I was able to bring
another body like my own
into a ruptured world.

Back then, I borrowed money,
a friend, and a crumpled
address in Ensenada,

and back then I was too naive
to worry my body
about complications.

Back then, I was still in recovery
from a religion insisting
there is no body.

Back then, it was all cloak
and dagger, a matter
of intrigue and disguise.

Back then, I was accustomed
to disguise, hiding
the body from the body.

On the return flight to Oakland,
I did not comprehend
the blood smeared

across my blouse, the aching
in my groin, the numbness
in my heart.

I turned to my friend beside me,
who put two fingers
to my lips:

Shush, don't tell!

Blood, Sweat, & Tears

If I had a daughter,
I'd tell her
You have a body.
It grows on you,
this body, this knowing
its ten orifices
open to the world.

If I had a daughter,
I'd explain how
the auditory canal
directs air waves
from outside
to the tympanic
membrane
conveying
electric energy
to the brain
to hear the planet
humming.

If I had a daughter,
I'd show her
the nares at
the entrance
to her nose
and the slimy
surface inside
collecting dust,
pollen, detritus
to keep these out

of her airways
and draw in
the living breath
of the earth.

If I had a daughter,
I'd want her to know
the whereabouts
of that crevice,
the conduit
to the uterus,
from where we
all come into being.

If I had a daughter,
I'd want her to recognize
that her words hang
in the air,
almost never
black or white,
that what comes up
from the windpipe
is the breath
of the trachea
vocalized
into what matters.

If I had a daughter,
I'd laugh and cry
with my mouth full
of the concerns
mothers have

for their daughters
in harm's way,
in the way
of the body
in this world.

If I had a daughter,
I'd tell her
it matters,
this body
that knows
its entrances into
and exits out
of the world.

But she'd already know.
The body always
knows, unless it's
been compromised.

Fragments

Some say the body is obsolete.
In seven years the cells retrench
into something else, the flawless skin
wandering back out of the sea.

*

How what we begin we only think
is ourselves, alone, together.
How quickly we separate, drift off
until we are some other life
threading the air.

*

I have a memory.
It swims deep in blood,
a delta in the skin. It carries my arms
and legs to these places: to the bottom
of a pool where I tried to save a boy
who did not make it, to the edge
of an island that surrounds me
with its mothball fleet of blood, hair,
and teeth hauling themselves out
of their long winter's sleep.

*

Maybe the body is what we are looking for
as evidence.

*

And I know I have seen Portola in 1767,
sitting high in the saddle
on Mt. Diablo, holding his hand
to his eyes, and looking out across the bay,
where anyone might be my father,
and I, anyone's daughter.

*

As I stride through the twenty-first century,
I wonder where else a child
could grow up denying
what it's like to be robbed
of solid weight and mass,
to be robbed of space,
to shiver in the indelible cold.

I Ring, I Round, I Rosie

I ring
       I round
              I rosie,

skirting the part
       where we lose
              our balance

at the edges
       of the world,
              where we are

only a jumble
       of bodies thrown
              into that ring.

But the game
       is not a song
              nor a sorrow,

and there's still time
       to wake ourselves
              to the illusion

of somewhere to go
       somewhere to hide.
              We ring, we round, we pose

our images in the mirror,
       pinch both cheeks
              to draw blood to the surface,

creating a rosy glow
      to prove we are still alive
            in this solid body of the world.

We ring, we round, we all
      fall down, stand back up,
            and do it all over again.

Naked Eye

In childhood photos, I am the one who is squinting
as if I'm in pain. As if pain were the only reminder

of being in the body. And here's a photo of the ruby-
crowned bird hovering outside my window as it feeds

on honeysuckle. Turns out hummingbirds don't suckle.
They drink the nectar. And they see colors we cannot.

In the photo, I do not appear at all, invisible to the naked eye.
But I know I'm there. If pain is an extra dimension of the body,

like the bird's extra cone detecting ultraviolet, it comes to light—
why I am still there. One morning, I found the body of the bird,

lifeless under the honeysuckle. As the bird dissolves into the past,
my naked eye sees something glimmering. Write it as grief.

The hand hovers in the air; the bird stays there.

Bits and Shards

More and more, I am writing
from another time and place,
one I remember
in bits and shards.

Broken pieces.
Sharp edges.

Or maybe it's a place
I've never known
or a time that has not yet
happened.

Wherever it is,
I am reluctant to leave,
as it offers all a body
needs to conjure wariness,

provided you are brave
like the Ukrainians
asserting their will
to stay alive.

After isolation,
after the unmasking,
fear gives way
to someone out there

singing across the dark,
remembering another life.

And *yes*, the body,
of course, the body

with its multitude
of decisions
and indecisions,
and *yes*

Notes on the Poems

P. 8

"I am afraid to own a body...Profound—precarious property"
is from Emily Dickinson's Poem 1090 in the 1960 edition of *The Complete Poems of Emily Dickinson* (Little Brown & Company, Boston).

P. 18

Homo ludens translates from the Latin to "Man the Player."

P. 31

Some art scholars think Leonardo Da Vinci is the basis for his *Vitruvian Man*. The artist was described as being well proportioned, muscular, and attractive, with curly hair to his shoulders. https://artfilemagazine.com/the-vitruvian-man-by-da-vinci/

P. 33

From 1958-1960, Edward Teller, father of the hydrogen bomb, was director of the University of California's Lawrence Radiation Lab in Livermore, where the author's father managed the high-pressure lab. In 1960, she was introduced to Dr. Teller on Family Day at the Lab and later took Physics for Non-Majors from Teller at UC Berkeley.

P. 47

Ion, a play by Euripides, was written between 414 and 412 B.C.

About the Author

Kathleen Ellis grew up in the San Francisco Bay Area, received her B.A. from University of California, Berkeley and M.A. from University of Maine, Orono. The author of *Red Horses* and three chapbooks of poetry, she has also translated poems by Latin American women, and co-edited *The Eloquent Edge: 15 Maine Women Writers.* She is the recipient of fellowships from the National Endowment for the Arts and the Maine Arts Commission, residencies from Yaddo and Djerassi, and the Pablo Neruda Poetry Prize from *Nimrod.* Poems from her manuscript, Dear Darwin, were set to music and released as a Parma Recordings CD, which was nominated for a 2015 Grammy Award. Ellis teaches poetry at the University of Maine, coordinates the annual POETS/SPEAK! event in Bangor, and lives in Orono on the ancestral lands of the Penobscot peoples.

CPSIA information can be obtained
at www.ICGtesting.com
Printed in the USA
BVHW030322180123
656425BV00029B/145